Checking In

A Semi-Functional Girl's Guide to Surviving the Psych Ward and Other Existential Crises

Kennedy Layne

Magnolia Ink

Copyright © 2026 by Kennedy Layne

All rights reserved.

No portion of this book may be reproduced in any form without written permission from the publisher or author, except as permitted by U.S. copyright law.

This publication is designed to provide accurate and authoritative information in regard to the subject matter covered. It is sold with the understanding that neither the author nor the publisher is engaged in rendering legal, investment, accounting or other professional services. While the publisher and author have used their best efforts in preparing this book, they make no representations or warranties with respect to the accuracy or completeness of the contents of this book and specifically disclaim any implied warranties of merchantability or fitness for a particular purpose. No warranty may be created or extended by sales representatives or written sales materials. The advice and strategies contained herein may not be suitable for your situation. You should consult with a professional when appropriate. Neither the publisher nor the author shall be liable for any loss of profit or any other commercial damages, including but not limited to special, incidental, consequential, personal, or other damages.

Book Cover by Sarah Conner, DMC

First Edition 2026

ISBN: 979-8-9935996-4-9

Also by Kennedy Layne

Honeyshore & Peach Cove Universe—
The Shelf Indulgence Chronicles:
The Tide Don't Break
The Rising Tide Rests
The Tide Burns Brighter
Chasing the Tide

Charmed by Love Series:
Charmed by the Chase
Charmed Under the Lights
Charmed by the Foundation

The Fate Bound Saga:
Bound by the Current

Non-fiction
CHECKING IN:
A Semi-Functional Girl's Guide to Surviving the Psych Ward and Other Existential Crises

Contents

Content Warning	VII
Mental Health Resources	IX
Dedication	XI
1. Handle With Care: Fragile Human Inside	1
2. Pre-Arrival Tips	3
3. Rule 1: Cry	9
4. Rule 2: Stay Away from Creeps	13
5. Confessional Break:	17
6. Rule 3: Relax	19
7. Confessional Break:	23
8. Rule 4: Stand Up for Yourself	25
9. Confessional Break:	29
10. Rule 5: Utilize Group Therapy	33
11. Rule 6: Do Not Let Nerves Cripple You	37
12. Rule 7: Confide in Others	41
13. Confessional Break:	45
14. Discharge Day: The Last Morning	47

15.	A Quiet Ending	49
16.	Bonus: The Sis Session	51
17.	Postscript	59
Acknowledgements		60
About the Author		62

Content Warning

This story contains sensitive subject matter that may be triggering for some readers. Please take care while reading.

<u>Topics addressed include:</u>

Mental health struggles

Suicide ideation

Self-harm

Psychiatric Hospitalization

If you're in a tender place, I encourage you to prioritize your well-being and read with care.

Mental Health Resources

If you or someone you love is struggling, please know there is help and support available:

United States: 988 Suicide & Crisis Lifeline—
Call or text 988, 24/7, for free and confidential support. 988lifeline.org

International Resources:
befrienders.org—Global suicide prevention and emotional support.

Other Helpful Resources:
National Alliance on Mental Illness (NAMI): nami.org
The Trevor Project (for LGBTQ+ youth): thetrevorproject.org

You are worthy of help. You are not alone. Healing is possible—and your story is not over.

Dedication

For the entire staff—medical, advocacy, cafeteria, administrative—and the patients of Coastal Harbor Health in Savannah, Georgia, who kept me safe and steady from May 3–11, 2018. You helped me rebuild from the inside out, even on the days when I could barely find my own pulse, let alone my perspective.

For my psychiatrist, Dr. Gbadebo, who somehow spotted the light buried in my dark long before I saw even a flicker.
(Truly impressive, considering I showed up looking like a plot twist.)

And for my therapist, K., who continually encourages me to shine through. Thank you for reminding me—again and again—that sometimes the sunshine we're waiting on is the sunshine we have to make ourselves…preferably with carrot cake (you'll get it by the end of the story).

Handle With Care: Fragile Human Inside

If my life came with a warning label, this would be it:
Handle with care. Contents under pressure. May cry without warning.

By the time everything cracked, I wasn't even surprised. I was just tired—of proving my worth, of pretending I belonged, of trying to smile my way through another day that felt too heavy to carry.

At the bank, I was the dependable one. The fixer. The person who could be counted on to do everyone's job when they "forgot." Which they often did. I trained new hires who were promoted over me, smiled at coworkers who gossiped behind my back, and swallowed every slight like it was my fault for not being tougher.

They called me "dedicated." I called it "overextended with a side of emotional decay."

The anxiety was constant—an uninvited coworker who refused to take PTO. Every Sunday, my stomach twisted itself into knots so tight I could barely stand. I cried getting ready for work. I cried *at* work. I cried in the car after work. Then I'd come home, run a hot shower, and let the water hide the sound of me breaking apart.

Sometimes I'd trace the edge of my wrist with a razor just to *feel* something—anything—that wasn't dread. It wasn't about wanting to die; it was about wanting the noise to stop. When people noticed the marks, I said my dog had scratched me. They nodded, half-listening, half-not caring. I was surrounded by people all day and still felt completely invisible.

Food became optional. My appetite packed up and left months before I did. I lived on Coke and Goody powders, half-fueled by caffeine and denial. Lunch breaks became fifty-minute naps in my car, cheek pressed against the head rest, praying I'd wake up feeling like someone else.

The night before the hospital, I sat on the bathroom floor, staring at my reflection through the steam. I looked like a ghost with a pulse—hair matted, eyes red, face hollow. I kept thinking, *if I could just fall asleep and wake up as someone else, maybe I'd finally be okay.*

But when I woke up, I was still me. Still tired. Still breaking. Still the fragile human inside.

Pre-Arrival Tips

How to Pack for Rock Bottom (and Other Practicalities)

THERE'S NO BUZZFEED QUIZ for *Which Savannah Psych Ward Are You?*—but if there were, I'd have scored a perfect match.

Mostly because when my psychiatrist said, "You're going for a short-term stay at a mental health hospital," I nodded like someone agreeing to a lunch date instead of a supervised stay in a locked facility. I was too tired to argue, too numb to panic properly. Somewhere in the back of my brain, a small sarcastic voice whispered, *Well, at least you'll finally get some sleep.*

By the time my dad arrived at the doctor's office to drive me home to pack, I'd melted into the soft sofa in the doctor's office like a discarded candle. Curled in the fetal position, crying softly behind the curtain my hair had created. The receptionist offered me a cup of water. I thanked her as if hydration might cure a nervous breakdown.

Packing for a Breakdown

No one tells you what to pack for a mental hospital. The brochure from my doctor's office wasn't much help—just vague warnings about drawstrings and contraband shoelaces.

I stood in my bedroom staring at an open duffel, thinking how surreal it felt to fold skorts and sleep shorts like I was going on a girls' trip when, in reality, I was heading for psychiatric purgatory.

My dad didn't come inside, tied up on the phone with one of my managers from work. My sister showed up with the efficiency of someone on a mission.

"Comfy clothes," she said, as I pulled my favorite pajamas from a drawer. "Nothing with strings or zippers or—what did they say?—underwire?"

I remember panicking because my favorite sleep shorts has a faux drawstring on them. My hands were shaking while I panic-talked my dad into cutting the bow off. It was probably an overreaction, but who the hell really knows?

We packed in silence—the kind thick enough to chew on. I grabbed soft socks like they were lifelines. I almost packed mascara, then laughed at myself. Mascara? For what? To look good while having an existential crisis?

I definitely should've thrown in some Summer Fridays or peptides lip balm, though. The generic jarred stuff they gave me was awful. A girl should at least know her limits.

When we were done, the bag looked like something a sad influencer might post with the caption *#selfcare*.

Pre-Departure Jitters

Before we left, I did one last sweep of my room, suddenly convinced I might never see it again. That's the dramatic thing about depression—it turns even the mundane into a potential farewell tour.

I glanced at my unmade bed, my dramatic teal walls, the dress I'd worn that morning strewn across the bed, the photo-booth strip of me and my sister at a Braves game making stupid faces. My chest tightened.

"I'll take care of Char," my sister said quietly.

"He has to sleep on his own pillow, ya know," I replied.

"I know. Your dog lives up to his name—Prince Charming."

She smiled, and I almost did too.

The Drive

The drive to Savannah was a blur.

I don't remember if the radio was on or if it was quiet. It might've been both—noise outside, silence inside. My sister drove, focused and calm, while I bit my bottom lip hard enough to taste blood just to keep from crying. Feeling embarrassed and ashamed.

I've never been good at going anywhere alone. I'm the kind of person who needs a friend for everything—doctor's appointments, Target runs, even oil changes. But this? This was different. I was being dropped off somewhere I didn't understand, by the people who loved me most, and they couldn't stay to save me.

The drive from home to Savannah isn't long, but that day it felt entirely too short. I just wanted a traffic jam, a detour, anything to prolong the destination arrival. But I was out of luck. The roads blurred into a watercolor of pine trees and billboards and the occasional gas station. The sun shone bright—too happy, too normal, for what was happening in my world. I tried to swallow the panic, but it sat heavy in my chest, humming like static.

My sister asked if I was okay once. "Yeah," I lied, staring at the horizon. "I'm fine." She didn't push. She just nodded and kept driving.

When we finally pulled into the parking lot on Stephenson Avenue, my stomach dropped so hard it felt like gravity doubled. The building looked beige and harmless from the outside—like an old office complex that didn't want to be noticed. I remember thinking, *That's where I'm supposed to get better? That's where I'll sleep tonight?*

My mom's car was already there. She'd driven in from Hilton Head, her sunglasses perched on her head, sun still clinging to her skin. She waved when she saw me, hopeful, like this was just another one of my appointments. I wanted to wave back, but my body wasn't cooperating.

Everything after that came in flashes:

- Gravel crunching under my shoes.

- My mom's arms wrapping around me, tighter than usual.

- My sister standing a few feet away, quiet.

- The doors opening with a loud buzz of electronic locks releasing, and the cool hospital air swallowing me whole.

For one last second, I looked over my shoulder. They were both still there—my mom and sister—standing together on the other side of the threshold. Then the doors closed, the locks slamming back into place, trapping me inside.

And just like that, I was alone.

Intake

The lobby was blindingly bright—white walls, white floors, white ceiling. The kind of sterile white that makes you feel like you're standing inside a lightbulb. There was a bulletin board plastered with pictures of former patients smiling with Sharpie-scrawled captions like *You got this!* and *Keep shining!* I remember staring at it and thinking, *Okay, but do they know I'm not exactly a "shiner" right now?*

It was quiet—no phones, no TV, no background music to soften the awkwardness. Just the air conditioner humming and me trying not to sweat through my favorite pajamas. My hands were shaking, which made filling out forms feel like taking the SATs during an earthquake.

The registrar—this calm, modern-hippie type—spoke in the kind of soft, reassuring tone that makes you think she probably drinks lavender tea and believes in the power of moonlight. Dressed in a comfy maxi skirt and tee shirt, finished with costume jewelry. I instantly loved her. She handed me a clipboard and pen that said *Be Kind to Your Mind*. Cute. I'd been trying to be kind to my mind for years. It just refused to return the favor.

Then came the indignities. I had to empty my cute Lilly Pulitzer duffel into a brown paper bag. Watching my colorful clothes plop in like groceries was…humbling. I know it's policy, but still—it felt like punishment with extra beige. They wouldn't let me keep my teddy bear either. Yes, a teddy. My emotional support bear. The registrar smiled sweetly and passed it off to my sister. I nodded but in my head I was like, *Ma'am, that bear has seen things. He's earned visitation rights.*

I handed my phone off to my mom before she and my sister left. Watching them walk toward the door felt like the end of the world's shortest road trip. I bit my lip until I tasted blood because if I cried again, I might never stop.

The nurse who took my vitals was funny—genuinely funny. She made a joke about my pulse rate being a roller coaster and told me I should be proud of "thriving under pressure." She was the first person all day who made me laugh.

Then came her evil twin—the intake orderly. Cold, fast, and allergic to joy. She fired off questions like she was speed-running an interrogation. When I tried to explain that I hadn't attempted suicide, that I'd been self-harming, she cut me off. "It's the same thing," she said flatly. It wasn't, and I asked her to change it, but she refused. By the time she finished, I felt more like an entry in a spreadsheet than a human being.

After that, I was running on autopilot. Someone slapped a wristband on me. Someone else pointed toward a door. I followed instructions like a lost extra in my own movie.

They led me to a common room where both the men and women waited before being assigned to wings. There was a TV tuned to *Family Feud*, a table of coloring books, and a radio faintly playing soft rock—because apparently mental breakdowns have soundtracks.

I started crying again. Not the dramatic kind—more like silent, leaking tears of exhaustion.

As they guided me down the hall, the electronic locks clicked behind us. Each one sounded final, like punctuation at the end of a sentence I didn't remember agreeing to.

And just like that, I was officially checked in.

Rule 1: Cry

(You're in the right place for it.)

If you think crying makes you weak, congratulations—you've probably never checked into a psych ward.

The second I crossed into the women's wing, I started crying again. No dramatic warning, no buildup—just immediate waterworks. It was like my tear ducts had been waiting all day for their big debut.

A volunteer guided me down the hallway, speaking in that calm, practiced voice that made me think she'd definitely seen worse. She showed me to my room, handed me sheets to make my bed, and promised that everything would be okay—that the tears would stop soon. I nodded, even though I didn't believe her, and the exhaustion hit like a sedative.

I lay down on the crisp white sheets that smelled faintly of bleach and something flowery pretending to be comforting. The tears kept sliding down, but the exhaustion won. Within minutes, I was asleep.

Two hours later, someone gently shook me awake and said it was time to "hang out in the common room with the other ladies." I assumed this was their version of social exposure therapy.

The common room looked like a middle school lounge that had been through a rough divorce. Wooden chairs with carpet-style cushions, worn coloring books, and a TV tuned to *Game Show Network*. I curled up in a small alcove, hoping to blend into the furniture. The tears started again—still quiet, the kind where your chest just trembles.

That's when she appeared.

An emo girl with black hair and a blanket draped around her shoulders like a cape. She walked over, handed me a tissue, and said in the most matter-of-fact tone, "You look like you're having a bad day, dude."

I half-laughed through the tears. "You could say that."

She nodded, then tucked her blanket tighter around me like we were suddenly in a sleepover. "We've all had bad days," she said. "It gets much better."

Then she walked away, leaving me with the tissue and the tiniest sliver of comfort.

Permission to Fall Apart

Everywhere else in life, I'd trained myself to hold it together—at work, at home, even in the doctor's office. I was the "I'm fine" girl. The one who smiled through panic attacks and apologized for existing.

But here? Crying wasn't a crisis. It was part of the process. No one flinched. No one handed me inspirational quotes or told me to "think positive." They just let me cry.

That night, I curled up under the thin blanket, the air conditioning blasting straight into my soul, and cried myself to sleep again. But it wasn't the same kind of cry. It wasn't hopeless anymore—it was tired, human, necessary.

Somewhere between the sobbing and the silence, I realized that maybe crying wasn't falling apart at all. Maybe it was the first thing I'd done right in a long time.

Between the Tears

That night, after lights dimmed and the hallways went quiet, I finally got to use one of the phone booths. The walls were this pale yellow that someone probably thought was soothing, but really just screamed government-issued optimism.

I called my parents first. My mom's voice cracked the second she heard mine. My dad tried to sound steady, like he was fine, like this was just another pit stop on the highway of life. My sister kept her voice bright, asking if I'd eaten, if I'd made any friends yet—as if this were college orientation.

Then I called Tillman. My best friend. My person.

He answered on the first ring and said, "Hey, friend." Just hearing that broke something open in me. I wanted to tell him everything—the fear, the crying, the girl with the cape—but all that came out was, "I'm okay, I think."

And I was, sort of. Happy, for the first time in weeks, to hear familiar voices. But also completely hollowed out. Like every emotion I'd ever had was sitting on the floor next to me, waiting its turn to be felt.

By the time I hung up, my throat hurt from talking and my heart felt wrung out like a dish towel. I crawled into bed, pulling the blanket up to my chin, my plastic wristband crinkling with every move.

For the first time since I'd arrived, the tears didn't come.

Not because I felt better—just because I had nothing left to give.

Rule 2: Stay Away from Creeps

(And maybe don't wear flip-flops.)

By the time I finished intake, I was starving in that "haven't-eaten-since-the-world-collapsed" way. The staff handed me a late lunch and pointed me toward the co-ed common room—a beige multipurpose space that smelled like Lysol and defeat.

I sat at a table by myself. One guy coloring at a table next to me. Everyone else seemed to be outside enjoying the sun.

I sat with my chef salad, trying to act like I belonged there, which is hard to do when you're clutching a paper cup of Thousand Island like it's holy water. It was my favorite dressing—so at least one thing in my life still made sense.

I'd just speared a tomato when I felt eyes on me. The prickly kind of stare that makes your shoulders tense before you even turn your head.

The guy at the other table (we'll call him *Chad*) wearing socks with sandals (a fashion red flag anywhere, a security alert here)—was watching me. Not blinking. Just…staring.

I glanced down at my tray, pretending not to notice. Maybe he'd lose interest if I ignored him. Spoiler: he did not.

In a sing-song voice, he said, "Your toes are cute. I like your toes."

I froze mid-bite. For the record, nothing—and I mean nothing—prepares you for toe commentary in a psychiatric institution.

I wasn't even barefoot. I had on flip-flops, the kind that pop every time you take a step, reminding you that your life choices have landed you somewhere with laminated safety posters.

My brain short-circuited. The only thought I managed was, *This is how I die*. I was going to be a documentary on *Investigation Discovery* or an episode of *48 Hours*... "The Lowcountry Toe Foe Strikes Again".

"Uh...thanks?" I said, because apparently my coping mechanism is south Georgia politeness.

The volunteer's head snapped up like she'd developed telepathy for awkward situations. "Hey *Chad*" she said cheerfully, walking over, "you know you're supposed to be on Quiet Time. Leave her alone. Let her eat in peace".

She handed me a fresh napkin. "Eat, breathe, rest," she said. "You've had a day."

She wasn't wrong.

I finished my salad in silence, listening to the hum of the fluorescent lights and my own heartbeat trying to slow down. The adrenaline crash hit all at once. My hands trembled around the plastic fork.

By the time she came back to check on me, I was glassy-eyed and barely upright.

"Let's get you settled in your room, honey," she said. "You look done."

I was. Completely.

I thanked God when she led me to the women's wing and the next volunteer took over from there, just as calm and comforting.

By the time the new volunteer showed me my room and said I could rest for a while, I was done.

My late lunch had ended with toe commentary and trauma—so yeah, nap time sounded divine

Refer to Rule #1 if you encounter any creeps

Confessional Break:

Core Memory—Carrot Cake

By day two, I'd realized the snack cart was the real heartbeat of the hospital. Forget therapy—snacks were the great equalizer.

I became a regular. My go-to order was a simple but dependable combo: chocolate pudding or chips from the cart with apple juice. Later, during visiting hours, a candy bar and a Coke from the vending machine. (A balanced diet, obviously.)

But my true love was dinner dessert—carrot cake. I chose it every single night without fail. It was moist, spiced, topped with thick cream-cheese frosting, and, I swear, probably responsible for fifty percent of my emotional recovery. I still talk about that carrot cake—to my family's complete and utter annoyance.

After months of living on Cokes and Goody powders just to quiet the hunger-headaches, feeling hungry again felt like a miracle. I hadn't realized how much joy there could be in wanting food. Every bite of that carrot cake tasted like coming back to life.

I'm sure the kitchen staff thought I was unhinged. But honestly? In a week built on breakdowns and breakthroughs, the highlight of my day was a slice of institutional carrot cake and the comforting hiss of a vending-machine Coke.

Healing doesn't always look like epiphanies under fluorescent lights.

Sometimes it looks like dessert.

They could keep their group therapy—I had frosting and caffeine.

Rule 3: Relax

(You're technically on vacation—just with more supervision.)

By Day 2, I'd learned two important things:

    1. Nobody cared if you cried anymore.

    2. There was such a thing as Quiet Time, and it was holy.

Breakfast that morning was eggs, bacon, toast, a banana, and grits. I had both coffee and apple juice—because why not live a little? It was the first full meal I'd actually wanted to eat in weeks.

I realized two things while sitting there with my school lunchroom tray:

    1. It was May 4th—Star Wars Day—and I didn't get to wear the cute themed dress I'd planned for work.

    2. It was also my first full day free of self-harm.

So technically, *the Force really had saved me.*

There was something grounding about that. Silly, yes, but comforting in its own nerdy way. The date stuck to me like a promise: *May the Fourth Be With You*, indeed.

I realized, somewhere between bites of banana and the last sip of coffee, that the world hadn't ended. My job was still out there, but for the first time in years, it wasn't my problem. My doctor had filled out my FMLA paperwork before I checked in. I was getting paid to rest, cry, and eat hospital bacon. Corporate America could wait.

It was like a very specific kind of spa retreat: no phones, no Wi-Fi, no deadlines—just group therapy, cafeteria food, and a mandatory bedtime. I could work with that.

The Art of Doing Absolutely Nothing

Once I'd survived my first 24 hours, the schedule started to take shape: vitals, meals, therapy, naps, repeat.

It was oddly soothing. There's a comfort in knowing what comes next, even if "next" is just more granola bars.

Between group sessions and nap time, we watched a *Star Wars* marathon on the TV in the common room. The room had turned into a galaxy far, far away—minus the lightsabers and plus an occasional nurse checking blood pressure.

It felt fitting.

The irony wasn't lost on me: a bunch of emotionally unstable adults watching a movie about redemption and rebellion in matching hospital socks. The Force, it seemed, really did work in mysterious ways.

Visitors and Vending Machines

Visiting hours were my version of happy hour. My mom and sister came every single day, armed with hugs, updates about Char, and stories from the outside world. Bringing bags of goodies: coloring books, books to read, and cozy socks. My dad stopped by some evenings, pretending not to tear up when I told him I was doing okay.

During visiting hours, we were allowed to use the vending machines in the cafeteria. I'd make a beeline for the Coke button like it was a pilgrimage. There's nothing quite like that first cold sip of real caffeine after 48 hours of water, juice, and hospital coffee.

Candy bars were my other vice. Reese's or Snickers. I swear they melted slower in there, probably just out of sympathy.

On Saturday—my third day—Tillman showed up, along with another friend from home, Garrett. Seeing them walk through those doors felt surreal, like the outside world had bent time to come visit. We sat at a table, talking and laughing about nothing in particular. It felt normal, which was maybe the most healing thing of all.

Finding My Pace

By the end of that first week, I'd stopped checking the clock so often. The days had rhythm now: group therapy, meals, naps, comforting tv shows and movies, visiting hours, repeat. I was eating again. Smiling sometimes. Even laughing at bad jokes.

I wasn't fixed. But I was fed, rested, and starting to feel like maybe I could exist again without coming apart.

Learning to Rest

Before the hospital, I thought resting meant laziness. That slowing down was weakness.

But somewhere between the *Star Wars* marathon, the naps, and the vending machine Cokes, I realized rest wasn't a luxury—it was survival.

For the first time in a long time, no one expected anything from me. I wasn't answering emails or fixing problems or proving my worth. I was just…breathing. Existing. Healing in the most boring way possible.

And maybe that's the point.

Healing isn't glamorous. It's naps and tears and soft food and tiny wins that no one claps for.

But sitting there in that quiet, fluorescent bubble, I started to believe something I hadn't in months—that maybe I was allowed to feel okay again.

Confessional Break:

Quiet Time (and Other Miracles)

They called it Quiet Time, but I called it : *my Super Bowl*

EVERY DAY AFTER LUNCH, we had a couple of hours where everyone was supposed to "rest." Most people used it to think, journal, or stare into the fluorescent void. I, however, approached it like a sacred ritual.

I napped. Hard.

Not polite, eyes-closed resting— full-commitment, REM-cycle-level sleeping. If snoozing were a competitive sport, I would've taken home the gold. Princess Aurora would've been proud. Honestly, she was my role model those nine days—minus the curse, plus the institutional-issue blanket.

Sometimes I'd wake up early—just long enough to color half a page or watch reruns of *Family Feud* in the common area—but mostly, I stayed wrapped in my blanket, blissfully unconscious.

It was the first time in months my brain wasn't on fire. The first time rest didn't feel like weakness.

Quiet Time was pure, uninterrupted peace—a small, padded miracle between therapy sessions and emotional breakthroughs.

It taught me that sometimes healing doesn't look like doing.

Sometimes, it looks like napping.

When Quiet Time ended, they expected us to talk about feelings again—which, frankly, felt rude.

Rule 4: Stand Up for Yourself

(Or at least stop apologizing for breathing.)

By Day Three, I'd realized the psych ward was basically a small town with bad lighting. Everyone knew everyone's business, and the staff floated through like sheriffs trying to keep the peace. Gossip traveled faster than the lunch trays, and someone was always crying in a hallway. Sometimes it was me.

Group therapy was mandatory, and as someone who hates talking in circles of strangers, I considered this a personal form of torture. The chairs were arranged in a loose circle, like a support group in a *Hallmark* movie—but with more nervous energy and less coffee.

Our therapist, an excited woman—who came off as a former cheerleader and probably younger than me—made us share what had brought us there.

No pressure.

I listened as a few people spoke—some shaky, some steady, some trying too hard to sound okay. When it was my turn, my heart was beating so loud I was sure it echoed off the walls.

"...I think I forgot how to stand up for myself," I said, mostly to the floor. "I let too many things break me down, and I didn't notice until it was too late."

There was a pause. The kind that feels like the whole room is holding its breath.

Then someone murmured, "Same."

Then another, "Yeah, me too."

And just like that, I didn't feel so ridiculous for saying it out loud.

Boundaries, But Make It Therapy

Another afternoon, the same group decided to talk about body image, body shaming, and weight. A few people started comparing diets, and I could feel the anxiety crawling up my throat. My brain whispered, *leave, leave, leave.*

So I did.

I quietly got up, walked out, and found my peace.

It felt rebellious and liberating—like ditching class, but emotionally healthier.

A volunteer followed me over to the common area asking what happened. I explained the topic made me uncomfortable and picked up a dot-to-dot book to take over to a table. Before I sat down a couple of other people followed me out of Group—apparently uncomfortable but too scared to leave at first. It was a powerful feeling knowing I helped others by advocating for myself.

The Small Victories Count

Standing up for yourself doesn't always look like a dramatic confrontation. Sometimes it's as simple as saying "no" to a conversation that hurts, or asking to take a nap in your room, or choosing carrot cake over Jell-O because texture is a real thing (and like, it's carrot cake obvi).

Each small act was a little rebellion against the version of me who always stayed quiet.

I was still scared most of the time—scared of saying the wrong thing, of being too much, of not being enough—but now there was this tiny flicker of something else, too.

Pride.

And maybe that's what recovery really starts with: not confidence, not certainty, but a small, stubborn spark of *I deserve to be okay.*

By the time group wrapped up that afternoon, I'd realized something big: standing up for yourself doesn't mean you're rude, or dramatic, or difficult.

It just means you finally stopped pretending you're fine when you're not.

So yeah—today I walked out of group therapy and chose carrot cake over Jell-O at dinner.

That might not sound revolutionary, but to me? It was progress.

Apply to Rule #5 as needed.

Confessional Break:

The Girl Who Said I'm Fine (Spoiler: She wasn't.)

Before I ever set foot in a psychiatric hospital, I was already fluent in one language—the art of pretending I was fine.

"I'm fine" was my default setting.

I said it to coworkers while silently falling apart.

I said it to friends who didn't notice the shake in my voice.

I said it to myself in the mirror, just to see if I could still sell the lie.

The girl who said "I'm fine" was the picture of composure—smiling, productive, reliable. She handled everything. Until she didn't.

She was the coworker who volunteered for the extra shift, the daughter who didn't want to worry her parents, the friend who sent "you got this!" texts while silently drowning.

She didn't mean to lie.

She just didn't know how to tell the truth without breaking open.

There were signs, of course. The crying-in-the-shower kind. The sitting-on-the-bathroom-floor kind. The kind where the sound of running water covers the sound of your own heartbreak.

I used to trace lines on my wrists when the noise in my head got too loud—marks from razors or scissors I could hide under long sleeves and cardigans. Sometimes I'd press hard enough to leave a scab, just to feel something again.

When someone noticed, I joked that my dog had scratched me.

"Char gets excited," I'd say, smiling too fast.

No one questioned it, which almost hurt more.

I thought I was protecting everyone from the truth. Really, I was protecting myself from being seen.

It took a hospital wristband and a week of supervised crying for me to realize "fine" isn't a goal. It's a mask.

The girl who said "I'm fine" wasn't weak.

She was exhausted.

She was lonely.

She was begging for someone to call her bluff.

And when someone finally did, it saved her.

I still say it sometimes—old habits die hard.

But now it means something different.

"I'm fine" doesn't mean "don't ask."

It means "I'm figuring it out."

It means "I'm still here."

These days, my sister can always tell when I'm lying; I blink or too much or avoid eye contact. Progress, apparently, is learning to tell on yourself with your eyes.

And honestly? That's enough.

Rule 5: Utilize Group Therapy

(Even if your therapist sounds like a motivational cheerleader on espresso.)

My first group therapy session was outside.

Apparently, sunshine is good for morale—or maybe they just wanted to make sure no one fell asleep mid-share.

We sat in a loose semicircle of benches facing a small courtyard fountain that made this polite trickling sound, like it was trying not to interrupt anyone's trauma. The sun was blinding. I squinted so hard my forehead started to ache.

I sat crisscross-applesauce-style on one of the benches, pulling at a thread on my pajama shorts, trying to look casual while silently begging not to be called on.

Our therapist was a woman who could only be described as a human motivational poster. She had the energy of a high school cheer coach—Torrance from *Bring It On* levels of pep—and clapped her hands every time someone said something vaguely positive.

"YES! THAT'S GREAT SELF-AWARENESS!" she'd shout, as if we'd just nailed a pyramid formation instead of admitting we cried in the shower.

She wore bright Converse and a headband that screamed *I do yoga at sunrise*. Her enthusiasm was…a lot.

"Let's talk about our goals for the week!" she chirped. "One thing you want to work on emotionally or mentally!"

I considered saying avoiding heatstroke, but decided to behave.

When it was my turn, I said, "I want to figure out how to stop spiraling every time someone emails me with the word 'urgent.'"

She gasped, delighted. "That's a wonderful insight! You're so self-aware!"

I wanted to tell her I was just self-exhausted, but I nodded politely instead.

The cheer-coach therapist kept the energy going like we were about to win regionals.

"Who wants to share first?" she said, clapping once for emphasis.

Naturally, everyone suddenly became fascinated by their shoelaces.

She scanned the group and landed on me—the girl squinting into the sun like a hostage.

"How about you, Kennedy?"

I could practically hear a drumroll in my head.

"Um… okay," I said, sitting up a little straighter. "I have borderline personality disorder."

Blank stares.

One woman tilted her head like I'd just spoken fluent Klingon. The fountain kept trickling helpfully.

The therapist beamed. "Thank you for sharing that, Kennedy! Would you like to explain what that means for you?"

I wanted to say, *No, not particularly*, but she was looking at me with that expectant pep-rally face, so I nodded.

"It's...complicated," I started. "Basically, I feel emotions like they're on speaker volume. I get attached too fast, I panic when people leave, and I'm really good at pretending I'm fine until I'm not."

Someone in the back said quietly, "Same." Another nodded.

And just like that, it wasn't as scary.

I told them how I'd been terrified to come here because of the way TV and movies make people with BPD look—*Fatal Attraction, Girl, Interrupted*, all that nonsense. The therapist listened, for once without clapping. When I finished, she said softly, "Thank you for teaching us."

That part hit different.

For the rest of the week, whenever the group circled up again, I didn't hide. I spoke. I asked questions. I even laughed sometimes.

Turns out, when you finally start telling the truth, people stop looking at you like you're broken—and start looking at you like you're brave.

See Rule 6 for additional encouragement.

Rule 6: Do Not Let Nerves Cripple You

(They already have medication for that.)

When the nurse told me the doctor wanted to meet with me that first night, my stomach dropped. It was close to nine p.m.—I was still shaky from the day, running on caffeine, fear, and sheer autopilot

She led me around the corner to a small office just off the women's common room. The light inside was soft but sterile, humming faintly like everything else in the building. The air smelled faintly of coffee and disinfectant.

The doctor was already waiting. Older—maybe in his fifties—with kind eyes and the sort of gentle smile that instantly reminded me of my Papa. He looked like someone who probably handed out extra peppermints at Christmas and meant it.

"Evening, Miss Kennedy," he said, standing to shake my hand before realizing mine were trembling and switching to a warm nod instead. "I know it's been a long day."

That was the understatement of the century. It had been a "long day" like World War I had been a "little disagreement".

He gestured for me to sit, and I sank into a squeaky vinyl chair that let out a groan of protest. He chuckled softly. "That chair complains more than my teenage daughter."

That made me laugh—an actual laugh, which startled both of us a little.

Then he started the standard intake questions.

> "Do you know where you are?"
> "Savannah."
> "Do you know what year it is?"
> "2018."
> "And who's the current president?"
> "Bush," I blurted.
> He raised an eyebrow. "That'd make my mortgage rate better, but no."
> I felt my face heat up. "Sorry. Nerves. I know it's Trump."
> "Understandable," he said kindly, jotting something down. "We'll mark that as 'momentary time travel.' Happens more often than you'd think."

Doctor's Orders: Rest

For the next fifteen minutes, he asked about my medications, sleep, eating, and thoughts. He never once made me feel like I was being judged. When I explained that I hadn't tried to end my life, that I was here because I'd been hurting myself and didn't know how to stop and plans of suicide never carried out, he nodded slowly.

"Thank you for telling me," he said. "You did the right thing coming here. You're safe now."

Something in his tone—steady, gentle, unhurried—untied a knot in my chest I didn't realize I'd been holding since that morning.

He stood to open the door for me when we finished. "Go get some sleep, Kennedy. We'll talk again tomorrow. Tonight, just rest. That's your only assignment."

The Thing About Nerves

Walking back to my room, I realized my hands had stopped shaking. My heart still raced a little, but the panic had faded into something softer—something like relief.

Maybe that's the trick with nerves. They convince you you're doomed until someone kind looks you in the eye and says, "You're safe."

That night, I crawled into bed, the hallway lights glowing faintly under my door, and for the first time since arriving, I believed it.

Apply to Rules 4 and 5 as needed.

Rule 7: Confide in Others

(It turns out vulnerability is a group project.)

By the end of my first week, I'd learned that healing wasn't something you did alone in a corner—it was something that happened between coloring pages, coffee refills, and inside jokes about institutional food.

Every woman in that wing had her own story, but somehow, they all overlapped with mine. We cried for the same reasons, laughed at the same absurdities, and found peace in the same small mercies—like quiet mornings or vending-machine Cokes during visiting hours.

Sometimes, in the middle of a conversation, I'd glance over at the alcove chair where I'd first met the emo girl with the black eyeliner and the superhero blanket. Her words still echoed: *"We've all had bad days. It gets better."*

She was right.

The tears still came, but they didn't hurt as much now. The laughter lasted longer. The quiet didn't feel like loneliness anymore—it felt like rest.

I wasn't fixed. I wasn't "better."

But I wasn't alone, either.

And maybe that was the whole point.

The Sisterhood of the Shattered Pajamas

The second night, during free time, a few of the women gathered around the coffee table in the common room. They were coloring, talking, passing around puzzles, and laughing about something I couldn't quite hear. One of them waved me over.

"You don't have to sit alone," she said. "We've got extra crayons."

That shouldn't have hit as hard as it did, but it did.

I joined them, and before long, I was laughing too—about nothing in particular, just the kind of laughter that fills the cracks. We traded hospital horror stories, snack preferences, and who'd cried in what room. It felt like the world's strangest sleepover, but it was exactly what I needed.

Learning to Lean

For the first time in months, I stopped worrying about being too much. I didn't have to edit myself or apologize for existing. Everyone here already knew what rock bottom looked like; they'd decorated it.

The next day, I started talking more—small things first. I told the women about my dog, Char, about my sister letting my be a passenger princess, about how my best friend Tillman was probably pissed I'd abandoned him at work for two weeks.

And in return, they told me their stories—messy, beautiful, broken ones that made me feel less alone.

The Moment That Stuck

One night, after lights out, I could still hear quiet voices from the hallway. Someone was being escorted into my room, to the empty bed. She was crying. The EMTs who brought her in told her to get some rest. I waited until the room was clear, as she settled in her bed, and softly said, "Hey, it's okay, we've all been there."

Those were the words the emo girl had said to me on my first day.

That's when I realized connection wasn't optional—it was medicine.

We came here for healing, but what really saved us was each other.

Confessional Break:

Cafeteria Therapy

Visiting hours were the closest thing we had to normal life.

Every afternoon, the heavy doors buzzed open, and the world from before drifted in—perfume, laughter, and bags full of goodies (mostly coloring books and cozy socks).

Each visit was a lifeline. For an hour, I wasn't a patient; I was just Kennedy again. We'd sit in the cafeteria at the long tables, talking about little things: what the dogs were doing, funny stories with other patients, visits from our therapy dog, Nala, and how much I missed chips and queso.

My family always brought me fun gifts. My favorites were the adult coloring and dot-to-dot books. The comfy socks and slippers were honorable mentions, obviously.

The perks of using the vending machines though, that was the real highlight. A cold bottle of Coca-Cola and a Snickers—psych ward equivalent of Heaven. I'd crack open a Coke and savor it like a fine wine.

They'd tell me about the outside world—how Char was sleeping on my sister's pillow every night, how my coworkers were asking about me, how my mom fell in the ditch riding a bike. I told them about group therapy, the carrot cake and the girl who called me "*dude*" when I cried.

We'd laugh, sometimes harder than we should have.

Every day, they'd hug me tight before leaving, and I'd feel that familiar ache—the one that says *please don't go yet*.

But even after they left, I wasn't as lonely anymore.

Their laughter stayed in the air a little longer each day.

Their love lingered like sunlight through the narrow windows, soft and steady.

Visiting hours didn't heal me overnight, but they reminded me why I wanted to be here long enough to try.

No one warns you that recovery comes with cafeteria chairs and vending-machine therapy.

Discharge Day: The Last Morning

(Spoiler: the real world still has fluorescent lights, too.)

The morning I was discharged, the world felt both familiar and brand new—like someone had wiped the fingerprints off my brain.

A nurse knocked gently before sunrise. "You're going home today, Kennedy."

Home. The word sounded strange in my mouth, like I'd forgotten how to use it.

I packed my things—a process that took all of five minutes, since I'd only brought a few pajama sets, lounge sets, socks, and emotional baggage. A new brown paper sack was now filled and folded closed, ready to go. Somehow, it didn't feel like punishment anymore. It felt like proof that I'd survived

My doctor did one last check in around seven, maybe eight. Same kind eyes, same crooked tie.

"You look better," he said, smiling.

"I feel...less like a haunted raccoon," I offered.

He laughed. "That's what we like to hear. Take care of yourself out there."

When my mom and sister arrived, I was full of smiles, no tears today. The sunlight outside was so bright it made me squint, and the warm air hit me like freedom.

The automatic doors opened, and this time, I walked through them on my own.

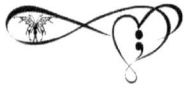

The Aftermath of Healing

We didn't go straight home. My mom declared that "a little retail therapy never hurt anyone," and my sister seconded it. So we spent the afternoon wandering down Broughton Street, weaving through boutiques and antique shops like tourists in our own state.

Everywhere smelled like perfume, sunshine, and possibility.

After that, we hit Oglethorpe Mall, because apparently my mom believed in exposure therapy through shopping. I bought my first pair of Lilly Pulitzer leggings and dress that day—a core memory for me.

We ended the day at a Mexican restaurant. I ordered enough food to feed a small army and ate until I could barely breathe. Chips, salsa, queso—the holy trinity of recovery. My mom kept watching me eat like she couldn't believe it. My sister kept smiling like she didn't want to look away.

For the first time in a long time, I didn't feel broken. Just full—of food, of laughter, of hope.

A Quiet Ending

That night, back in my own bed, Char curled up beside me and snored like a tiny freight train. The house was quiet, the lights dim, the air soft.

I still felt fragile. But I also felt alive.

The hospital had been cold and bright and full of strangers who somehow became my lifeline. I'd gone in terrified and left still uncertain—but lighter. The locks had clicked behind me again, but this time, I wasn't the one trapped.

There's no BuzzFeed quiz for *Which Savannah Psych Ward Are You*?

But if there were, I'd still pick mine.

Because it saved my life.

Bonus: The Sis Session

Filed under: Things We Don't Realize We Survive Together

Some memories arrive in bright, cinematic clarity. Others come back foggy and out of order, like someone dropped a handful of Polaroids and you're trying to piece together which one came first.

This chapter is both.

It's the story of a week neither of us expected to live through this young. It's the story of a drive, a cafeteria, some plastic utensils, a lot of fear, and a surprising amount of carrot cake.

But mostly, it's the story of two sisters realizing how tightly their lives were braided together—even when everything was coming undone.

The Day Everything Tilted

I didn't come home from the psychiatrist's office with a neat little treatment plan. I came home with news.

My sister was quietly texting, trying to understand, when I told her I was being admitted.

I stood in our hallway upstairs, waiting for her to come get me. The same hallway we slammed doors and screamed across. The same hallway where we whispered secrets about guys and swapped hoodies without asking.

Except that day, everything felt tilted.

She hadn't been in the psychiatrist's office with me. She didn't hear the doctor say the word *admitted*. But she heard it from me. And that was enough.

When I asked her later what was going through her head in that moment, she didn't add theatrics or soften it with platitudes.

> **"I was sad that you were feeling so low that you needed such an intervention. I was really sad that you'd be gone for a time and not right across the hallway. And I was worried…because I had no idea what the mental hospital would be like or if you'd hate it or be scared."**

She said it simply, but it landed hard—like she had quietly carried that fear for years without setting it down.

There was no meltdown, no dramatic music. Just two sisters standing still on the linoleum floor in a boring kitchen where the world had tilted to one side.

And then she grabbed her keys.

The Drive to Savannah

There is a certain kind of silence only siblings know. The kind that fills the space when everything hurts but neither person wants to say something that will make it worse.

That's the silence we took with us out the front door and into her car.

No suitcases. No dramatic airport scene. Just me holding an overnight bag on my lap like it was a flotation device, and her gripping the steering wheel like she was keeping us both tethered to the road.

When I later asked her how it felt, driving me to a place none of us had ever seen inside, she said:

"It felt heavy and sad…but I knew you needed the help."

The sky? No idea.

The music? Could've been Taylor Swift, could've been silence, could've been an AM radio preacher yelling about eternal damnation—we genuinely don't know.

Trauma edits scenes like a ruthless film director, cutting everything except the emotional core.

She remembers our mom crying as she signed my paperwork that morning. She remembers her brain "checking out." She remembers wanting to cry but not wanting me to see.

But she also remembers this: Even though she was scared, she drove. She showed up. She took me to the place that terrified her because *not* taking me was more terrifying.

We don't talk about courage like that enough.

Walking In

The building itself wasn't scary. It looked like a medical office that had lost to the color beige in a tragic accident.

But the unknown was loud.

The lobby smelled like disinfectant and whatever soap hospitals buy in bulk. My sister said later:

> **"It felt sterile...and the fact that we couldn't see the inside worried me."**

Honestly, same.

An intake worker called my name. I stood. My family stayed seated.

For the first time in my life, I saw my sister look small—like someone had reached in and gently folded her in half.

Her memory of that moment is burned in her mind:

> **"Watching you walk through those doors...I didn't know if you'd come out better or more traumatized."**

Movies really did us dirty with their portrayal of psychiatric hospitals. If only they'd shown the carrot cake.

Cafeteria Visiting Hours

If you've never experienced visiting hours in a behavioral health facility cafeteria, picture this:

A school lunchroom. Big, rectangle tables. Conversations held in murmurs because everyone's trying not to cry in public.

And the food? It was...vending machine snacks.

My sister remembers the big tables. My plastic utensils complaints. The way she kept asking if the food was decent.

> **"You complained about the plastic utensils lol."**

(She says "lol" out loud. It's a sister thing.)

What she remembers most is how I *looked*:

> **"You looked amazing—glowing and happy. You were already back to your bubbly self. I hadn't seen that in quite awhile."**

It took a mental hospital to de-fog my personality. Plot twist of the century.

There was a moment—she doesn't remember the exact day—when she heard me on the phone and thought, *There she is. She's coming back.*

> **"Oh absolutely. I could hear it on the phone...but seeing it in person was amazing."**

Midweek Miracles

Every recovery story has that moment—the shift from "maybe" to "probably."

For us, it was laughter.

She said seeing me laugh again made her feel hopeful. Made her certain she'd get her sister back. That whatever swallowed me didn't win.

She also remembers the part that surprised her most:

> **"That you actually loved the facility and the people. You said they were all so sweet to you."**

I did. And they were. And that mattered.

Discharge Day

The day I walked back through the doors, she said the first thing she saw was:

> **"Most definitely the big smile on your face."**

The second thing?

The welcome-home gift she and our mom had hidden in the car. I cried. Obviously.

She said she was "extremely happy" to have her sister back. And only now, years later, do I understand how much space my absence took up in her life.

She told me:

> **"I worried about how people were treating you and that I couldn't stand up for you."**

That's love in its purest form. Protectiveness that doesn't know what to do with itself.

The Week That Changed Us Both

When I asked what memory she holds onto most, she didn't choose the scary part. Not the doors closing. Not the moment I walked away. Not the cafeteria.

She chose understanding.

> **"The advice on how to handle things you go through with BPD...I didn't take it as seriously until after I knew you were hurting yourself. You always put on a big front trying to seem happy. It helped me see others more...even when they don't show it outwardly."**

That's the quiet legacy of that week. It made her more observant. More open. More willing to look past the surface of the people she loves.

It made both of us different in ways that make our family stronger.

What We Keep

Here's the truth:

This chapter isn't about the hospital. It's about sisterhood.

It's about the person who met me in the kitchen when I came home with news. The person who drove me into the unknown. The person who sat across from me at a cafeteria table with plastic utensils and hope in her eyes. The person who saw me coming back before I felt myself return.

Some people say recovery is a solo journey.

But I think sometimes it's two sets of footsteps—one shaky, one steady—moving in the same direction until both are strong again.

And if this book has a vault track, a secret track, an after-credits scene…

It's this:

Every story deserves a sister like mine.

Postscript

(In case you ever find yourself here, too.)

When I left the hospital, I promised myself I'd never forget what it felt like to be that scared, that small, that desperate for proof that life could still be okay.

If you're reading this and you've ever felt that way—like the world is too loud, your thoughts too heavy, or your heart too tired—please know you're not alone. You're not broken. You don't need fixing. You just need gentleness, time, and maybe a vending machine Coke.

Healing doesn't happen in a straight line. Some days it looks like progress. Other days it looks like crying in the shower, or laughing in group therapy, or eating an unreasonable amount of Mexican food because you finally can again.

If you've ever felt like you were too much or not enough, here's the truth: you are exactly enough, just as you are.

And if you ever have to start over—even if it's in a place with buzzing lights and plastic wristbands—it's still starting over.

May the Fourth be with you. Always.

Acknowledgements

WRITING THIS BOOK MEANT opening doors I once closed quietly and firmly. It meant revisiting a version of myself I never expected to meet again. But I didn't walk that road alone—not then, and not now. These pages exist because of the people who held me up when I couldn't stand on my own.

To my sister—
My first friend, my hallway confidante, my forever mirror. You drove me into the unknown when I needed help, but more importantly, you stayed. You showed up with hope, honesty, and the kind of love that steadies a person from the inside out. Thank you for seeing me before I could see myself again.

To Tillman—
For being the voice of reason, the safe place, the one who never lets me forget who I am—thank you. Your friendship is stitched through every honest moment in this book.

To Garrett—
Thank you for recognizing what I couldn't name in myself and for taking me to get help. You told me once that my weaknesses were strengths in disguise. I didn't believe you then. I do now. I'm grateful every day.

To everyone living with Borderline Personality Disorder or any mental health struggle—

I see you. I believe you. I'm walking with you. You are not your diagnosis. You are not too much. You are not alone.

To the people who love someone with BPD—
Thank you. Your patience, gentleness, and willingness to learn make survival possible. This book is as much yours as it is ours.

To the readers—
Thank you for choosing to spend time in these pages. Thank you for sitting with the messy parts, the soft parts, the painful parts, and the healing parts. Stories only matter when someone receives them with an open heart, and you did that. I'm grateful for you.

To Statesboro Psychiatric Associates—
Thank you for giving me a safe beginning when everything felt like an ending. Thank you for offering dignity, direction, and a path forward I could not see.

To my First Southern National Bank family—
You taught me that I could be the one who fills the world with sunshine—that my spirit was not something to apologize for, but something to share. I carry that lesson with me every single day.

And finally—
To the version of me who survived that week:
Thank you for staying. Thank you for choosing to keep going. Thank you for giving me a future to come home to.

This book is yours.

About the Author

KENNEDY LAYNE IS AN aspiring writer with a heart full of stories and dreams of sharing them with the world.

She's a proud dog mom to the cutest Maltese on the planet, Prince Charming (Char, for short), and a wild, rambunctious mini Golden Doodle named Presley Grace (yes, like Elvis).

Deeply rooted in her community, Kennedy is active in several civic organizations and volunteers as a librarian at her church library. She lives in south Georgia, with her younger sister, just down the road from her parents and her childhood home.

Kennedy is always planning her next adventure, whether it's a beach getaway or a magical escape to Walt Disney World. She's a proud Swiftie who believes there's a Taylor lyric for every occasion, that iced tea with Splenda (because, you know…diabetes) can cure anything, and that there will never be a better show than *The Vampire Diaries*. She cheers loudest for the Atlanta Braves and her beloved Georgia Southern Eagles—Hail Southern!

www.ingramcontent.com/pod-product-compliance
Lightning Source LLC
LaVergne TN
LVHW010607070526
838199LV00063BA/5105